THE GREAT COLORADO

Activity Book

rising moon

The Great Colorado Activity Book
© 2007 by Rising Moon
Illustrations © 2007 by:
Joe Boddy: 24-25
David Brooks: 13, 14, 16, 29, 34, 35, 39, 40-41
Mike Gordon: 15, 42
Peter Grosshauser: 3, 6, 8, 9, 10, 31, 37
Larry Jones: 4, 7, 11, 12, 18-19, 21, 28, 32-33, 48
Joe Marciniak: 27, 38, 43, 45, 46, 47
Don Rantz and Beth Neely: 36
Chris Sabatino: 5, 17, 22, 23, 26

www.risingmoonbooks.com

Composed in the United States of America
Printed in China

Edited by Kjirsten Wallace
Designed by David Alston

FIRST IMPRESSION 2007
ISBN 13: 978-0-87358-921-5
ISBN 10: 0-87358-921-1

Printed in Huizhou, Guangdong, PRC, China January 2016

Colorado Picture Puzzle

Use the pictures below to name some of the areas you might visit in Colorado.

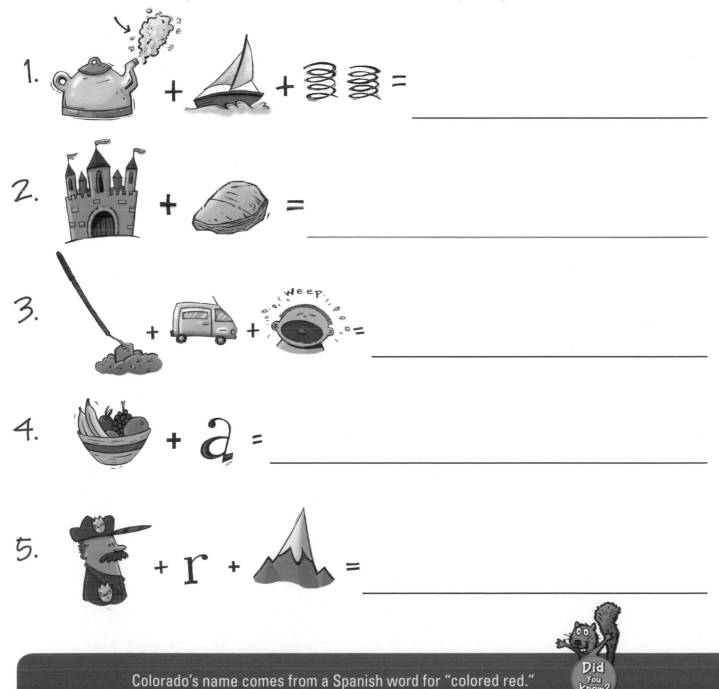

1. + + = _____

2. + = _____

3. + + = _____

4. + a = _____

5. + r + = _____

Ski Town Summer Fun

Horses and hiking and hot air balloons! Oh my! These folks know there are activities-a-plenty in Colorado's mountain towns, even when there's no snow. Which car do you think will end up in each resort area?

Some of these folks aren't respecting nature. Circle 7 things that these careless hikers are doing wrong.

5

My Rocky Mountain Vacation

You and a travel buddy can create your own version of your Colorado vacation.
① Don't let your buddy see this page and don't read the story out loud—yet.
② Ask him or her for words to fill in the blanks of the story. Use the words below the blanks as a guide.
③ When you've finished, read the story out loud and find out just how crazy your vacation could actually be.

This summer _____ and I went to Rocky Mountain National
(person's name)

Park. You wouldn't believe how big the _____s are there. When I
(type of animal)

looked out the car window, there was a/n _____ _____
(an animal)   *(–ing word)*

right at me. Maybe it wanted my _____. We know better than to
(a food)

_____ the animals though, so we just kept _____.
(action word)   *(–ing word)*

At our campsite, we pitched our _____ tent. It rained that night,
(describing word)

and I got _____. The next morning, I was really _____
(describing word)   *(describing word)*

and missed my _____. It was okay, though, because we saw
(things)

_____, who loaned me some. Having them inspired me to
(person you admire)

_____ all the way to the top of Long's Peak!
(action word)

Wolf Creek Ski Run Racers

Look out below! Lead these racers down the Waterfall Gully ski run.
Only one of them will make it to the finish line. Who will it be?

FINISH!

Skiers and snow-boarders from all over the world come to Colorado for the sunny days on fluffy powder.

Great Sand Dunes!

In the dune below, find the words describing what you might see at Great Sand Dunes National Park and Preserve.

```
              Y Z A B
            R E I L L A M
          D S E R A U M L L E
        C O T T O N W O O D S T P
      S R E P G S E S R R E O A I S
      W A W I N D A A F X A T S N D H
    N M E G L T G I L P C G W V O G D P
    A R L T T R R M R D L R A N G R Q A
  L W A D J L D U N E E N E V B F E T E N H
  L I K N T C S A V N B S B T A L L G W R D H A
F H H G G A H E N A D E O E R Z A P F E S E O E
P I L E N I U K C D A R N S F N T K E C B N C S A
A M E R O S I O N N S V A I Q T S E G D M A I R S T
N G Y N S N R U J O P H E B O P U B A C K P A C K I N G
T L T D A F L Z A P A T A F A L L S B E H W D N E R S U
S A N D C A S T L E G N L E R L V E E U E L B E I A S T C
O A S L D S E K I B E A S D V M E D A N O C R E E K I N O C
P W I N I J R V R N N Z R X G A L L M O A L L R I N R D O S
```

HIDDEN WORDS

BACKPACKING, BALD EAGLE, COTTONWOOD, DUNE, EROSION, MEDANO CREEK, PINON FLATS, PRESERVE, RANGER, SAND CASTLE, SANGRE DE CRISTOS, TUNDRA, WETLANDS, WIND, ZAPATA FALLS

PLEASE DO NOT FEED WILDLIFE!

Did You Know?

The park boasts North America's tallest sand dunes, some rising 700+ feet. Visitors can sled, ski, or surf down the massive dunes!

8

What's in a Name?

Can you match each of the Colorado places with a sentence below?
No joke—these names appear on Colorado maps!

1. ___ **BLACK FOREST**
2. ___ **SUGAR CITY**
3. ___ **DINOSAUR**
4. ___ **DIVIDE**
5. ___ **HYGIENE**
6. ___ **SECURITY**
7. ___ **YELLOW JACKET**
8. ___ **LOVELAND**
9. ___ **WILD HORSE**
10. ___ **RABBIT EARS PASS**
11. ___ **LAKE CITY**
12. ___ **LEADVILLE**
13. ___ **STEAMBOAT SPRINGS**
14 ___ **NORTH POLE**

A. You'll feel safe here.

B. Each year thousands of Valentines are re-mailed from this city.

C. What's up, Doc?

D. Sort of like the lost city of Atlantis, is it all under water?

E. I thought trees were green!

F. Do you have to be good at math to live here?

G. I hope it doesn't "spring" a leak!

H. "Santa! I've been very, very good!"

I. Oh boy, I didn't think these guys had been around in the last million years…

J. Sweet! We should stop here for dessert!

K. Come here to refill your pencil.

L. Buzz. Buzz.

M. Whoa, Bessie!

N. Brush your teeth and wash behind your ears.

State Symbols Crossword Puzzle

Test your Colorado knowledge. Use the state symbols and emblems listed below to fill in the puzzle.
HINT: Some of the vowels have already been filled in to get you started.

ACROSS

2. Colorado's state insect, the Colorado _____ Butterfly, lives at high altitudes.

4. The _____ is believed to have roamed Colorado lands 150 million years ago, so it is the state fossil.

6. Named for its silver-blue color, the Colorado _____ is the state tree.

7. You may not pick more than 25 of Colorado's state flower, the Rocky Mountain _____.

8. The _____, Colorado's state bird, returns annually to the state's plains in April.

DOWN

1. 100 years after the signing of the Declaration of Independence, Colorado became a state. Therefore, its nickname is the _____ State.

3. You might be called to "do-si-do" during Colorado's state folk dance, the _____.

5. The state fish, the _____ Trout, was almost endangered, but can now be found in streams and lakes.

9. Rocky Mountain _____, the state animal, climb the cliffs along mountain highways.

Bighorn Sheep, Blue Spruce, Centennial, Columbine, Greenback Cutthroat,
Hairstreak, Lark Bunting, Square Dance, Stegosaurus

Two-Wheelin' to Work

It's Bike to Work Day in Boulder. Help Jade pedal safely through her neighborhood on her way to the office. Don't forget to stop for the free breakfast she earns for doing her part in saving the environment!

Colorado's Native Americans

Use the names of the Colorado tribes listed below to fill in the puzzle. When you have them all, you should be able to name a great Ute chief, after whom a Colorado town, county, parks, and more are named.

How much do "Ute" know about Chief _ _ _ _ _ _ _ ?

(fill in the answer to puzzle)

✳ This chief and his wife Chipeta were known as keepers of peace.

✳ He was a well-respected leader and met with Presidents Hayes and Grant.

COLORADO TRIBES: ANASAZI, ARAPAHO, CHEYENNE, SHOSHONE, UTE

_ _ _ _ _ _ O _ _

O T _

_ O P _ _ _

_ _ S _ _ _

_ _ _ _ E

▲

ANSWER

Did you know this about Colorado's American Indian tribes?

- Horses were an integral part of Comanche culture.
- The Utes were known for beautiful beadwork and crafts.
- The Apache tribe participated in the rain dance.
- You can visit the cliff dwellings of the Anasazi Indians at Mesa Verde.

Did You Know?

Colorado Springs Postcard Conundrum

Oh, goodness! Your postcards from "the Springs" got mixed up. Can you straighten things out by drawing a line from the picture on the front of the postcard to the matching note on the back? Fill in the blanks to make sure they get to your friends and family.

Dear __Gigi__,

After our day at the zoo, we zipped down the hill to the Broadmoor Hotel for dinner. Famous people often stay there!

Sincerely,

Hudson

60673
YOKM
_____

Dear __Mi__, Mi

Many of the sandstone rocks in Garden of the Gods are over 300 million years old. That's older than your great grandma!

Love,

ygs

Htx
_____
91

Dear __miss fr__

We toured the planetarium and Cadet Chapel at the U.S. Air Force Academy. Way cool architecture!

Miss You,

missfr

Ag
_____
Hies

My Favorite Memory

Draw your very own favorite memory of Colorado. It's like taking a picture.

Wildflower Word Find

In Crested Butte, Wildflower Capital of Colorado, some of the most beautiful flowers and plants bloom every year. Can you find a few in the puzzle below?

```
P A S E Y S A L I E I T P N S R E P
E S Y L I R C P L S A H L E T L L Y A
N S R F K L G L A C I E R L I A E L P
S R Y E T G A S I R M E I L I A E P U
T Y A T H H E F N R L G P P U R N T P
E T A S I C E T T I E Y T L G C T N I
M K P S V O M B O E T T S E R A I N N
O I W T X I L R F A M E G L L F R O E
N N E L N W P U L N C U S L H F L E O
F N P E R B U S M L C U C S I I E R L
N I T E U M R H U B F P P E S E M A N
A Q R F A I R Y S L I P P E R M I W A
R S M E I T U K P E I N S K R I W N E
N U E R W K H L L I N N E I C N X E L
A F A S P E N S U N F L O W E R S H U
P L B F S L E M A B G I E H W T T L B
N A U O A T P D A I H F D N S B U A
A C W O R L E M I N E R S S O C K S
```

Columbine

Lupine

Glacier lily

Paintbrush

Fairyslipper

Elk thistle

Penstemon

Aspen sunflower

Scarlet gilia

Miners' socks

Fireweed

15

Round 'em Up

HOWDYPARTNER

Help this cowboy round up these stragglin' words. Each word has one spot in the puzzle above. See if you can get them all in line. **HINT:** The spaces between the words don't count.

Cattle drive
Stirrup
Campfire
Horseshoe
Brand
Bedroll
Lariat
Buckaroo
Chuck wagon
Guitar
Vaquero

16

CRAZY CAMP

These campers haven't decided how to conquer Pikes Peak tomorrow—by foot, train, bike, or car. They should really be concentrating on their tent instead. Number the scenes below to show what happened first, second, and so on during the family's camping trip in Colorado Springs.

Rocky Mountain Maze

Explore the sites of Rocky Mountain National Park. Keep your peepers peeled for sheep as you proceed. Don't forget to stand astride the Continental Divide and snooze under the stars at the campsite.

SHEEP LAKES

VISITOR CENTER

START! ➤

Sir Chomps O'Lot

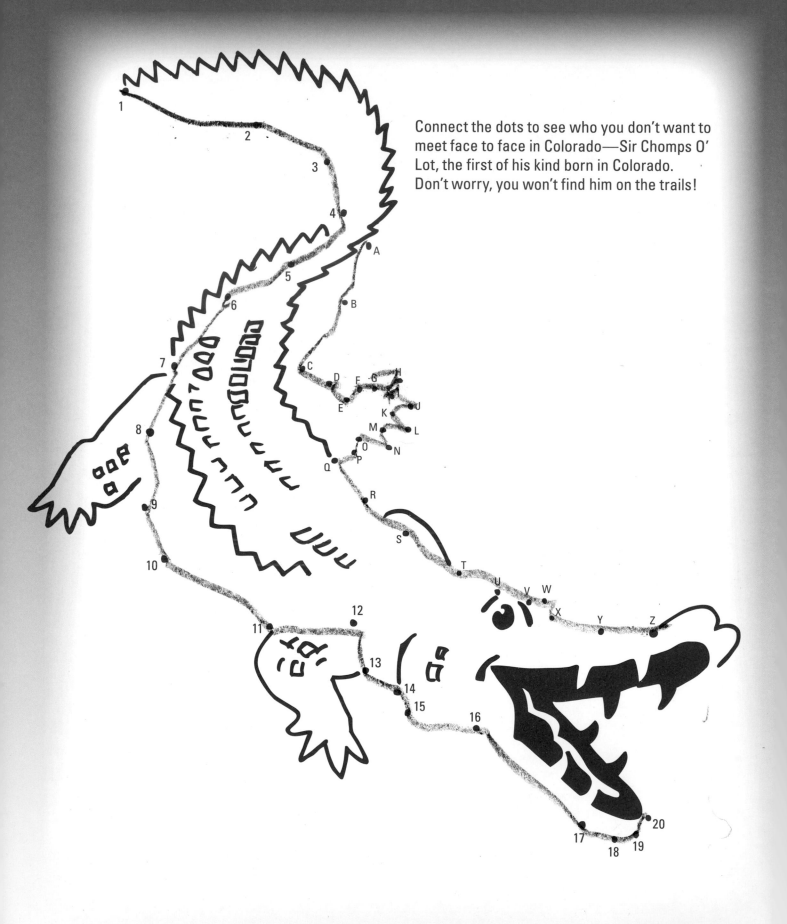

Connect the dots to see who you don't want to meet face to face in Colorado—Sir Chomps O' Lot, the first of his kind born in Colorado. Don't worry, you won't find him on the trails!

Trappin' and a-Tradin'

Find out more about an important landmark in Colorado trading history—Bent's Old Fort. Below, each sentence about the fort contains a picture clue. When you see a picture, write the word it represents into the corresponding space in the crossword grid. **HINT:** the first word is filled in for you. 1-Down is "FORT."

BUFFALO, SLEEP, CORN, WATER, INDIANS, BARRELS, TURKEY, RIVER, WAGONS

DOWN

1. Bent's Old **FORT** was established in 1833 along the Santa Fe Trail.

3. Travelers could get their repaired by the fort's carpenters.

4. A nearby water source for Bent's Old Fort was the Arkansas

5. During the war in 1846, the U.S. government stored military supplies including blankets and at the fort.

7. Visitors staying at Bent's ate meals of wild , deer, and elk.

ACROSS

2. The trade room stocked clothing, kettles, ,and more for sale or trade.

3. Bent's provided good drinking out on the plains.

6. The fort was built as a place to trade with Plains and trappers.

8. Native American tribes traded robes at Bent's Fort.

9. Weary travelers could at Bent's Fort.

The Bakers are staying at the elegant Stanley Hotel while vacationing in Estes Park. It's said strange things can happen at the Stanley. Just take a look at these two family portraits. Can you spot ten differences between them? Circle the differences on the bottom picture.

22

Blue skies and snowy summits are obvious, but can you spot the guitar, apple, compass, sunglasses, hiking boot, watch, footprint, lasso, camera, and water canteen hidden within this Dillon Reservoir scene?

Dinosaur National Monument Maze

Don't step on any dinosaur bones as you wind through this paleontological site to reach your tent.

START

Finish

At Dinosaur National Monument you can see dinosaur fossils, ancient pictographs, and petroglyphs.

Rocky Mountain Animal Scramble

These Rocky Mountain National Park critters are all mixed up!
Unscramble the names of the animals below. Have you seen any of them on your trip?

1. tocbba _____

2. osemo _____

3. elmu erde _____

4. hrogibn ehpes _____

5. tba _____

6. tmramo _____

7. ebarev _____

8. kel _____

9. dowo grfo _____

10. gnirtaamp _____

PARK ANIMALS

BAT ✷ BEAVER ✷ BIGHORN SHEEP ✷ BOBCAT ✷ ELK ✷ MARMOT ✷ MOOSE ✷ MULE DEER ✷ PTARMIGAN ✷ WOOD FROG

When a marmot is scared, it lets out a high-pitched whistle to warn other marmots in the area.

Did You know?

A Long Day on Long's Peak

Help these climbers view Rocky Mountain National Park from its tallest point, the top of Long's Peak! To reach the summit and be back down before the afternoon thunderstorms, they must hit the trail before dawn...yawn!

Did You Know? Long's Peak's summit is over 14,000 feet above sea level.

SOMETHING'S FISHY!

Maybe the silver's been mined, but there's a lot more to do in Silverton. In the nearby Wimenuche Wilderness, you may catch some weely whoppin' fish! Can you follow the lines to see which fish each fisherman caught?

Hot Springs
Mix-Up

In the white bubbles on each picture, number the scenes below to show what happened first, second, and so on during the Nelsons' trip to the hot springs pool in Glenwood Springs.

POOL

SORRY
No Pets

Welcome to
Glenwood
Springs

Did You Know?

Long ago, the Ute Indians bathed in Glenwood Springs' "healing waters," which bubble out of the ground at 122 degrees before being cooled and pumped into the pools.

All Aboard!

Connect the dots to learn where you can find one of the best views in Colorado

HINT: Open air or behind glass on the Durango & Silverton Narrow Gauge _ _ _ _ _ _ _ _ _.
Once you're done, you can color the scenery too!

A roundtrip, 7 hours traveling time,
uses 10,000 gallons of water!

Did You Know?

ANIMAL TRACKS MAZE

These animals left their tracks behind.
Match the bison, the coyote, the elk, and the bear with the correct set of tracks.

Denver Days

Denver has so much to do! Charlie visited many sites, but he needs to label the pictures before he forgets where he went. Can you help him match the captions to the pictures? When you find the right picture, write its caption number in the space below the photo.

CAPTIONS

1 Denver Zoo
The big cats were my favorite part.

2 Denver Botanic Gardens
Oh, the flowers!

3 Denver Art Museum
Never touch the paintings.

4 Denver Museum of Nature and Science
That T-Rex was over 3 times my height!

5 Colorado History Museum
Settlers in the 1800s didn't have all-wheel drive.

6 Molly Brown House
Glad I know how to swim!

Denver Zoo: Visitors to the Kimodo Dragon exhibit can get nose-to-(glass-to)-nose with these man-eating reptiles that can grow up to 10 feet long, and weigh 250 pounds!

Denver Botanic Gardens: The Denver Botanic Gardens presents beautiful flowers, concerts, fitness walks, art shows, a corn maze, and that's not even all of it.

Denver Art Museum: The American Indian art collection includes over 18,000 works, and is known as one of the best in the USA.

Denver Museum of Nature and Science: T-Rex and IMAX and galaxies galore! Mummies and minerals and mammals and more!

Colorado History Museum: Take a look at life in Colorado through the experiences of Native Americans, settlers, 10th Mountain Division soldiers, famous and infamous personalities, and others.

Molly Brown House: You can walk inside the restored house of Margaret Brown, known after she survived the sinking of the Titanic as "Unsinkable Molly Brown."

Royal Gorge Riddle

Use the symbols to discover one of the amazing things you can do at the Royal Gorge Bridge and Park.

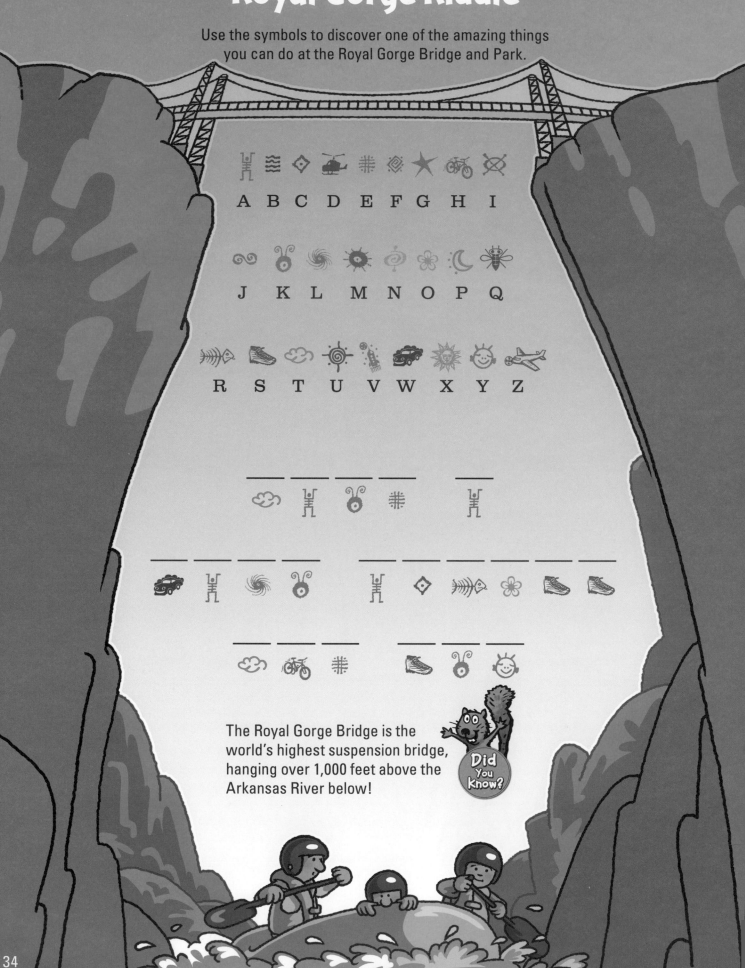

The Royal Gorge Bridge is the world's highest suspension bridge, hanging over 1,000 feet above the Arkansas River below!

Did You Know?

Don't Forget Your...

Colorado's mountains and valleys offer so much to do, you may not have time to try all these adventures in one outing. Try your luck at matching the equipment with its corresponding activity; draw a line connecting the two.

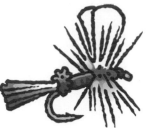

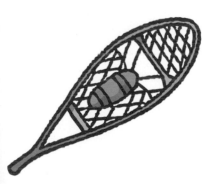

Hiking
Kayaking
Fly Fishing
Horseback Riding
Rock Climbing
Wildlife Watching
Skiing
Whitewater Rafting
Biking
Snowshoeing

Step Right Up!

Climb the ladders and scale the walls as you venture into the ruins of Mesa Verde from one end to the next. Don't pick up any ancient artifacts along the way!

FINISH

START

DON RANTZ
BETH NEELY '01

For hundreds of years Ancestral Pueblo people lived in communities in and around Mesa Verde, which means "green table" in Spanish.

Raging River Rafters

Help these rafters recover the items that fell out of their raft into the chilly Colorado River. See if you can find the sunglasses, cooler, soda can, sandal, swim trunks, hot dog, guitar, frying pan, tent, fishing pole, sun hat, suntan lotion, and flashlight in the picture below.

Hot Springs!

Whew! Those hot springs are hot. Help Laura get back to her family so they can all head up to the picnic area for some cool beverages.

Strawberry Park Hot Springs is open year-round. Even after a long, winter day on the ski slopes at Steamboat, you can bathe in the hot water, with the snowflakes falling all around!

Panning for
Gold!

CRIMINY! Clear Creek is full of treasures! This gold panner has picked up more than just gold. Can you sort through his collection to circle the peanut, screwdriver, worm, and fishing hook?

Gold can still be found today in certain areas of Colorado.

Did You Know?

Colorado Travel Bingo

Bingo is the name of the game-o. On your road trip through Colorado, try this. You and another player each pick a board. Look out your window, and mark the picture on your board if you spot it outside. The first person to spot five things in a row—down, across or diagonally—wins!

Fun Things to Do in Colorado

Crossword Clues

DOWN

2. Pitch your tent and _____.
3. So many curios shops. Let's go _____.
5. Put on your boots and take a _____.
6. In the winter you can go downhill or cross-country _____.
8. You can learn to be a cowboy at a dude _____.
11. After all this fresh air, I'm starving. I could _____ a whole pizza!
13. You might strike it rich. Pan for _____.

ACROSS

1. Pull out your camera and take lots of _____.
4. Learn about the history of Colorado by visiting a _____.
7. Spend some time with nature. Visit a National _____.
9. Cast your line and go _____.
10. Giddy up! Spend the day _____-back riding.
12. You're going to get wet on a whitewater _____ trip.

Cram-Packed Climber's Pack

Roy the rock climber was a little too prepared. The contents of his pack are spilling all the way back to Ouray! Can you pick out a frying pan, Roy's dog Daredevil, the kitchen sink, glasses, a light bulb, and a flower vase?

Today Ouray is known as the "Switzerland of America," and its beauty attracts visitors of all kinds. In years past, it was a mining town. Nearby you can visit the ruins of numerous ghost towns.

Did You Know?

Colorful Colorado

An unofficial nickname for the state is *Colorful Colorado*. It just takes a quick glance out the window to see why. Use your colors to bring the beauty of this scene to life.

Boo! I found you!

Can you find the mining pick, ghost, bucket, hat, jug, tombstone, boot, horseshoe, hair bow, fork, nail, hanger, bottle, wagon wheel, candle, and shovel hidden in this ghost town?

Hi-Ho-Hi-Ho

Colorado towns like Leadville, Georgetown, and Idaho Springs are rich with mining history. Help this miner strike gold. Can you dig up the words in the mine below?

BAD AIR   ORE   BAKED POTATO METHOD   TOMMYKNOCKER   CARAT
DREDGE   NUGGET   ADIT   SHAFT
POKE   CACHE   VEIN   SLUICE
PLACER DEPOSIT   PANNING
FLUME

```
F F T O M M Y K N O C K E R D L T I O
G L A G C D E H F C U L N S R K G T U B
P A U E H S T F M R I L O N H A D C R U B S
L T I M V L N A T S E T M E K A I R T U B S
A V S G E U M U M B A D A I R S F T H E
C A D U A I D M G O G T E U A K P T E A V
E S O A R C E A R G H C M S N P P K T A V E
R G E D E E T B O R E F E O B U A T V E
D E Y K N A I R T O R T R E B L N F E I N
E M A C D E D F A D E B L W F E N O I N
P N D O R H S C K M N D A S E T I N N R G
O Y D O E R A P O K E N D L R R N E R G
S K H A D F L N A D O R I K G I G D E G
I F I K G K H M S H P R T E E R S S O E
T O C B E R C E M A C A R A T H D A O D
E L B A K E D P O T A T O M E T H O D E
T D I L C E T N V R H G O I R C P G E
S V T F A H Y E O R N E A N L E N F T
D T O O N R E R U T S Y M I Q V B I A
```

Leave No Trace

This is an important rule to remember
when you're out on the trail.
Use the symbols below to get the message.

GET ALONG L'IL DOGGIE

Help! This poor prairie dog must find which tunnel leads to his cozy den below before the hungry hawk snatches him up.

Colorado Scavenger Hunt

Now that you've completed *The Great Colorado Activity Book*, take a minute and revisit some of the fun you had. Go back and find each of the items below within these pages. Mark the page number beneath the picture. How many of these things did you really see in Colorado?

Solutions

COLORADO PICTURE PUZZLE
(Page 3)

1. Steamboat Springs
2. Castle Rock
3. Hovenweep
4. Fruita
5. Copper Mountain

SKI TOWN SUMMER FUN
(Page 4)

TROUBLESOME TRAILBLAZERS
(Page 5)

WOLF CREEK SKI RUN RACERS
(Page 7)

GREAT SAND DUNES!
(Page 8)

```
                    Y  Z  A  B
                 R  E  I  L  L  A  M
              D  S  E  R  A  U  M  L  L  E
           C  O  T  T  O  N  W  O  O  D  S  T  P
        S  R  E  P  G  S  E  S  R  R  E  O  A  I  S
        W  A  W  I  N  D  A  A  F  X  A  T  S  N  D  H
     N  M  E  G  L  T  G  I  L  P  C  G  W  V  O  G  D  P
     A  R  L  T  T  T  R  R  M  R  D  L  R  A  N  G  R  Q  A
  L  W  A  D  J  L  D  U  N  E  E  N  E  V  B  F  E  T  E  N  H
  I  K  N  T  C  S  A  V  N  B  S  B  T  A  L  L  G  W  R  D  H  A
F  H  H  G  G  A  H  E  N  A  D  E  O  E  R  Z  A  P  F  E  S  E  O  E
A  M  E  R  O  S  I  O  N  N  S  V  A  I  Q  T  S  E  G  D  M  A  I  R  S  T
N  G  Y  N  S  N  R  U  J  O  P  H  E  B  O  P  U  B  A  C  K  P  A  C  K  I  N  G
T  L  T  D  A  F  L  Z  A  P  A  T  A  F  A  L  L  S  B  E  H  W  D  N  E  R  S  U
S  A  N  D  C  A  S  T  L  E  G  N  L  E  R  L  V  E  E  U  E  L  B  E  I  A  S  T  C
O  A  S  L  D  S  E  K  I  B  E  A  S  D  V  M  E  D  A  N  O  C  R  E  E  K  I  N  O  C
P  W  I  N  I  J  R  V  R  N  N  Z  R  X  G  A  L  L  M  O  A  L  L  R  I  N  R  D  O  S
```

50

WHAT'S IN A NAME?
(Page 9)

1.	E	8.	B
2.	J	9.	M
3.	I	10.	C
4.	F	11.	D
5.	N	12.	K
6.	A	13.	G
7.	L	14.	H

STATE SYMBOLS CROSSWORD PUZZLE
(Page 10)

TWO-WHEELIN' TO WORK
(Page 11)

COLORADO'S NATIVE AMERICANS
(Page 12)

1. Shoshone
2. Ute
3. Arapaho
4. Anasazi
5. Cheyenne

How much do "Ute" know about Chief **OURAY**?

COLORADO SPRINGS POSTCARD CONUNDRUM
(Page 13)

WILDFLOWER WORD FIND
(Page 15)

```
P A S E Y S A L I E I T P N S R E P
E S Y F K I R C P L S A H L E T L Y A
N S R Y F L L G L A C I E R L I L Y L
S R Y A E H K T G A S I R M E I I A E P
T A H H E H F N N R L L G P U R N T U
E M K P S I C E T T I E Y T S E C A I P
M O N I W E X O M B O E T T S E C R A I R
O N N E L N W P U L N N I A I R S R E O
F P P I T E U M R H U B F P P E S I H F L
N I T E U M R H U B F P P E S I H F E E
A Q R F A I R Y S L I P P E R M A R R
R S M E I T U K P E I N S K R I W E N
N U E R W K H L L I N N E I C N X E H
A F A S P E N S U N F L O W E R S H L U
P L B F S L E M A B G I E H W T T S U
N A U O A T P D A I H F D N R S B S U
A C W O R L E M I N E R S S O C K S
```

SOLUTIONS

ROUND 'EM UP
(Page 16)

TRAPPIN' AND A-TRADIN'
(Page 21)

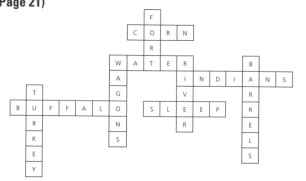

CRAZY CAMP
(Page 17)

DOUBLE EXPOSURE
(Page 22)

ROCKY MOUNTAIN MAZE
(Page 18-19)

HIDDEN AT DILLON
(Page 23)

A LONG DAY ON LONG'S PEAK
(Page 27)

DINOSAUR NATIONAL MONUMENT MAZE
(Page 24-25)

SOMETHING'S FISHY
(Page 28)

ROCKY MOUNTAIN ANIMAL SCRAMBLE
(Page 26)

1. Bobcat
2. Moose
3. Mule Deer
4. Bighorn Sheep
5. Bat
6. Marmot
7. Beaver
8. Elk
9. Wood Frog
10. Ptarmigan

SOLUTIONS

HOT SPRINGS MIX-UP
(Page 29)

ANIMAL TRACKS MAZE
(Page 31)

ALL ABOARD!
(Page 30)
Railroad

DENVER DAYS
(Page 32-33)

ROYAL GORGE RIDDLE
(Page 34)
Take a walk across the sky

DON'T FORGET YOUR...
(Page 35)

Hiking
Kayaking
Fly Fishing
Horseback Riding
Rock Climbing
Wildlife Watching
Skiing
Whitewater Rafting
Biking
Snowshoeing

STEP RIGHT UP!
(Page 36)

RAGING RIVER RAFTERS
(Page 37)

FUN THINGS TO DO IN COLORADO
(Page 42)

```
        P I C T U R E S
        A           H
M U S E U M         O       H
        P           P       I
              S     P A R K
        R     K     I       E
        A     I     N
        N   F I S H I N G
        C     N
        H O R S E     G
        A           A
        R A F T I N G
                    O
                    L
                    D
```

CRAM-PACKED CLIMBER'S PACK
(Page 43)

HOT SPRINGS!
(Page 38)

BOO! I FOUND YOU!
(Page 45)

PANNING FOR GOLD!
(Page 39)

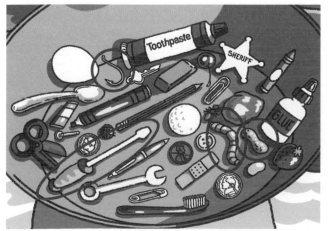

SOLUTIONS

HI-HO-HI-HO
(Page 46)

```
F F T O M M Y K N O C K E R D L T I O
G L A G C D E H F C U L N S R K G T U B
P A U E H S T F M R I L O N H A D I R S
L T I M V L N A T S E T M E K A R T T H
A V S G E U M U M B A D A I R S F T E E
C A D U A I D M G O G T E U A K P K A V
E S O A R C E A R G H C M S O B U I P E
R G E D E T B O R E F E O N T F O N I I
D E Y K N A I R T O R T R E B L A V E N
E M A C D E D F A D E B L W F E I T N R
P N D O E R H S C K M N D L A S E T I O
O N Y K H A D F L N A D O R I D K G I G
S I F I K G K H M S H P R T E E R S E D
I T O C B E R C E M A C A R A T H A A O
T E L B A K E D P O T A T O M E T H O D
E T D I L C E T N V R H G O I R C P G N
S V T F A H Y E O R N E A N L E N F T A
D T O O N R E R U T S Y M I Q V B I A
```

LEAVE NO TRACE
(Page 47)

Take only pictures. Leave only footprints.

GET ALONG L'IL DOGGIE
(Page 48)

COLORADO SCAVENGER HUNT
(Page 49)